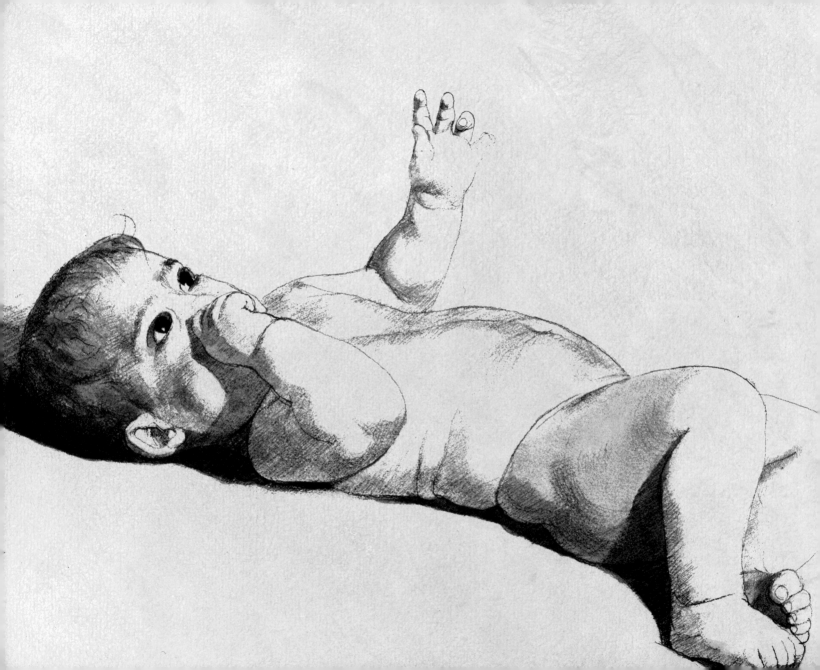

The wonderful
story of
how you were born

by Sidonie Matsner Gruenberg

with illustrations by Symeon Shimin

Doubleday & Company, Inc.
Garden City, New York

For my grandchildren:

Peter Barnard	Katheryn Mary
Daniel Barnard	Jean Allee
Nicholas Benjamin	Judith Sidonie
Elizabeth Allee	Joel William
Richard Joseph	Matthew Alan
Ann Matsner	Richard Matsner

and my great-grandchildren:

Joshua David	Rachel Stephanie
David Mark	Beth Ann
Madeline	Jenifer

Acknowledgments: I want to express my deep appreciation for all the help I have received in revising this book, first published in 1952, in order that it can effectively serve the present generation of boys and girls: To my brother, Dr. Eric Matsner, Fellow in the American College of Obstetrics and Gynecology and a leader in the field of maternal and health education, with whom I worked very closely on this edition; to my colleagues at the Child Study Association of America for many helpful suggestions; to my daughter, Hilda Sidney Krech, who is a professional writer and has been co-author with me on a number of projects, for her valuable assistance; and to Helen Puner who collaborated with me in the preparation of the manuscript of the original edition.

Designed by Earl Tidwell

The wonderful story of
how you were born

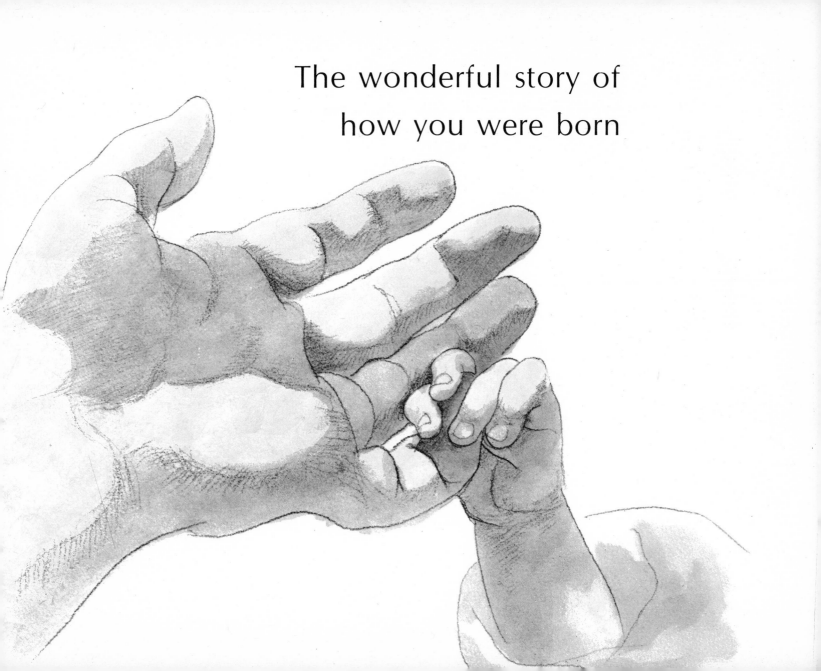

Do you remember when you were a baby? Do you remember when you slept all day and woke up only when you were hungry? Do you remember when you couldn't walk, when you crawled on your hands and knees? When you couldn't even stand up unless you held on to something?

But of course you don't remember that far back. *No* one
remembers being a baby. The only reason you know you
were once a baby is that sometimes you have seen pictures
of yourself or have heard stories about what you were like
when you were very little.

When you look at a picture of yourself taken last year, you may think, "Yes, that's the way my hair goes," or, "I remember those shoes."

But when you are shown a picture of a newborn baby, isn't it hard to believe that the little tiny baby was you?

No matter how long each of us has lived or how many children we may have seen grow up, it still is hard to believe that we were once children ourselves. And that before we were children, we were babies—newborn babies. This is something that everybody wonders about now and then.

That's why we love to look at old family pictures, pictures taken at different times. They remind us of the way everyone grows and changes each year. We all change and yet we stay the same; we keep on being the same person.

Do you wonder about that too? Do you wonder how that picture of a girl can really be your mother when she was young? Can that picture of a boy really be your father before he grew up? And that picture of a little two-year-old—can it really be you?

Now that you are big, you may think, "I can *do* so much and *say* so much and *think* so much, I can't believe I was ever a tiny newborn baby!"

"How can that be?" you say to yourself. "And *where*," you wonder, "was I *before* I was born?"

These are questions that boys and girls all over the world have always asked. But sometimes it is hard to get an answer. You see, most parents used to believe that children simply didn't think about such things as how babies are born, or couldn't understand them.

And so they often made up different kinds of stories about it. Sometimes they would say the baby was found under a cabbage leaf, or came in the doctor's little black bag. Or in some countries they would say the baby was brought by a big white stork.

But now we realize that children *do* think about themselves and *can* understand the true story of where babies come from. And the true story is far more interesting than any made-up story.

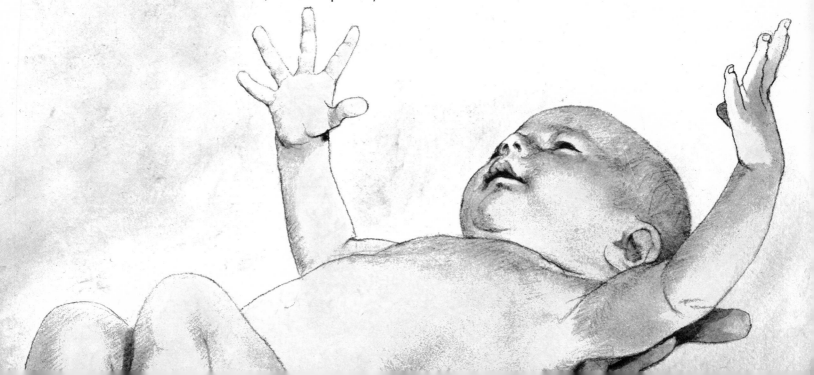

It is part of the whole story of how all living things keep on coming into the world. For not only does every person have a beginning, so do all kinds of living things around us—the birds, and the fish, and all the other animals, and every plant.

This is a story people have wondered about for a long, long time. Yet it is always new to each one of us.

At the beginning, you were no bigger than a dot, much smaller even than the dot on this page, or a single grain of sand. You were like a tiny little round egg, so small that it could not be seen at all, except through a microscope.

You began from a tiny egg cell in your mother's body called an *ovum,* joined with something else—even tinier—from your father's body. This something else was a special kind of cell called a *sperm.*

When a single sperm cell has combined with an egg cell, we say the ovum has been *fertilized.* A brand-new *fertilized ovum* was the very beginning of you. And even though it was so very small, that fertilized ovum had in it the whole plan for the special way you would grow.

Everybody you know started to be and started to grow from just such a fertilized ovum. Your mother did and your father did, and so did your sisters and your brothers, and all your other relatives and friends. No matter how big anyone is now or how small, he started to grow in exactly the same way. No matter whether a person has white skin, or black skin, or yellow skin, whether he lives in America, or India, or Africa, or China, he began as a tiny fertilized ovum.

Almost every living thing started out as a fertilized egg or seed, too. All the furry animals you know—from the biggest bears to the smallest mice. And all the insects, birds, and fish—all of these started from a tiny fertilized egg cell. And every kind of flowering plant, every vegetable, and every tree started from a tiny seed.

But even though so many living things began from a fertilized egg cell or from a seed, each one is different. Each new plant and each new animal grows to be the same kind of living thing as its parents.

There once was a little girl whose family already had three children but no pets. When she heard that her mother was going to have another baby, she thought it would be more fun if her mother had a kitten instead.

But of course her mother *couldn't* have had a kitten. People can have only human children like yourself and your friends. Dogs can have only puppies, and cats only kittens. Pine trees can make only the seeds that grow into other pine trees, and robins only the eggs that grow into robins.

So the tiny ovum that you began from was a very special and wonderful kind of egg cell. It couldn't have grown into a puppy, or a bunny, or a cucumber. It couldn't have grown into a kangaroo, or a cockatoo, or a duck-billed platypus. It could only have grown into a human being like you.

And your very special way of growing—from a baby sleeping all day in a crib to a big boy or girl running out to play and learning to do so many different things—was right there in the tiny fertilized ovum you began from!

Almost from the time you started to grow, the fertilized ovum that was you lay inside a special place in your mother's body. This place is called the *womb*. Another name for it is the *uterus*. It is shaped like a pear and is in the lower part of the abdomen. That's where you lived for nine months—the time it takes for human babies to get big enough to be born.

All this time you needed food and you needed air—for you were alive, even though you weren't yet born.

You got the food and you got the air through a kind of cord that connected your body where your belly button now is with the inside of your mother's womb. Of course you didn't have chicken and ice cream the way you do now. But you *did* get all the kinds of food and the air you needed for growing.

And so the first home you ever had was your mother's womb. It is a fine place for an unborn baby. There the baby is kept warm even if the mother walks through a snowstorm. For the inside of the womb is always warm, just like other parts of the human body. And it's always the same warmth —just right for the baby.

Also, the unborn baby isn't easily bumped or hurt, even if the mother should get bumped or fall down. For the baby inside the womb lies curled up in a bag of watery fluid. And this fluid acts like a springy cushion between the baby and any bump or fall the mother might accidentally have.

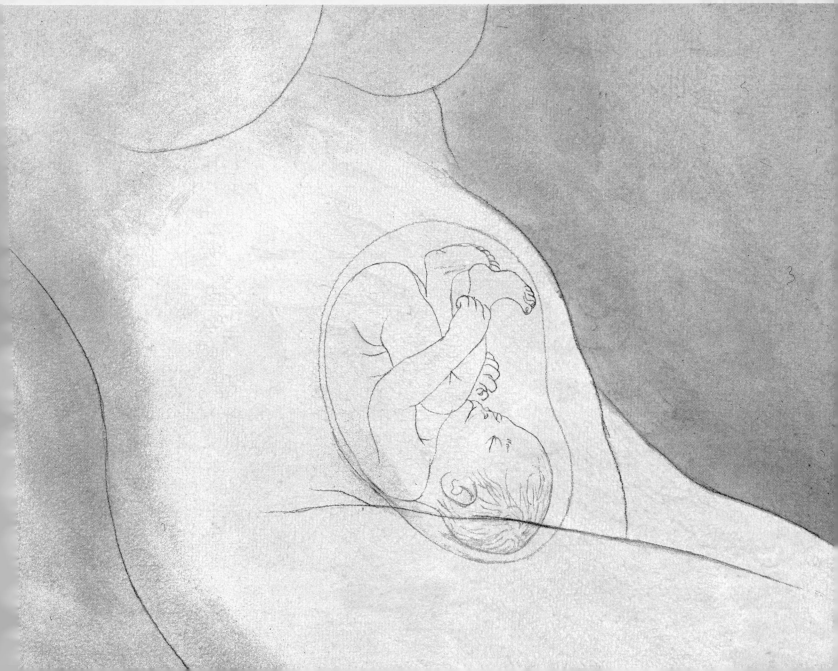

The tiny fertilized ovum that was you grew larger and larger—and larger. And as it grew, it slowly began to change its shape. After a few weeks of growing, you looked something like a funny little curled-up fish. But you were still very small, no larger than a tiny pebble.

So you kept on growing month after month. You kept on changing your shape. Soon you began to look more and more like the babies you've seen. Arms and legs began to develop. Eyes and ears and nose appeared. All the parts were forming that make up a complete little baby.

As your body got bigger inside your mother, her womb stretched and grew larger too, so there was always room for you. Your mother's breasts also grew larger. They were getting ready to make milk to feed you after you were born.

And after about four or five months of growing—about as long as it is from Thanksgiving to Easter, or from the Fourth of July to Halloween—you began to stir and move a little inside your mother's body. From the tiny fertilized ovum you had been, you had grown and changed so much in this time that you were able to move your arms and legs! No, your stirring and moving didn't hurt your mother. She was probably pleased and excited when she felt you moving about inside of her. It is one of the happiest, most wonderful feelings a mother has.

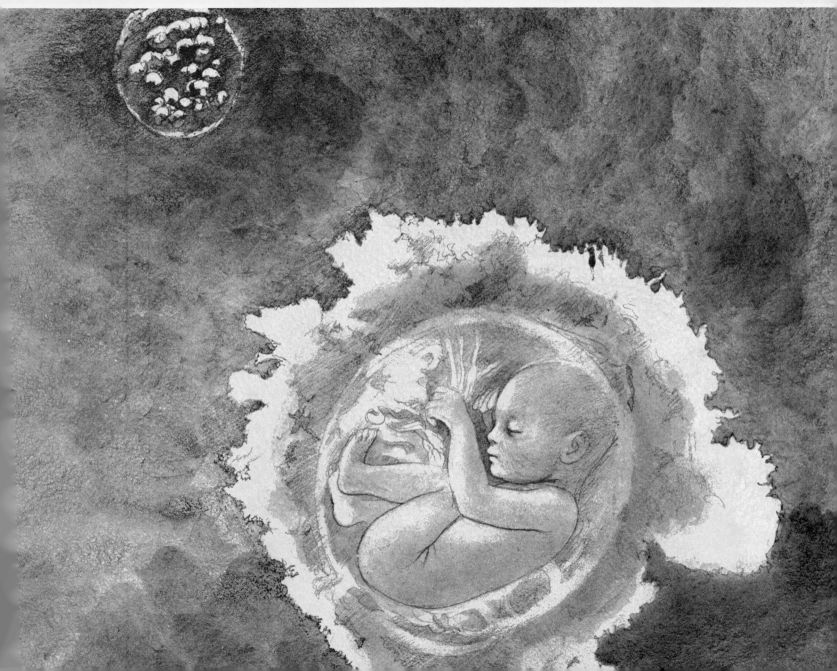

Your mother knew that in a few more months you would be ready to be born. She knew that then she would have either a little girl or a little boy of her own. Fathers and mothers wait eagerly for the great day to come when their baby will be born!

All their friends were waiting to see what you would look like. Would you be a boy or a girl? Would you have lots of baby hair or be almost bald with hardly any hair at all? Would you look like your mother or like your father—or a little bit like both of them?

Meanwhile, your family was getting ready for you. There was probably a special place to sleep prepared for you. And special clothes the size of dolls' clothes waiting for you to wear.

And while everybody was getting ready for you, you were getting ready for the great day, and your mother's body was getting ready too.

Inside the womb the baby's head lies close to the passage to the outside. When the time came for you to leave your mother's body, an amazing thing began to happen. The wall of her womb had been stretching and stretching as you were growing. And then—when you were ready to be born—it stopped stretching. Instead, the muscular wall of the womb began to push the baby that was you down into the *vagina*, which is the narrow passage to the outside. The vagina stretched too. From the vagina you got outside your mother's body—and so into the world. That's the moment you were born!

Some babies take longer to get born than others. Some take only a few hours, others take a whole day or more. Have you ever heard your mother say whether you took a long time or a short time to be born?

In this country most babies are born in a hospital because this is usually the most convenient place for a mother and baby to get all the attention and care they need. But this doesn't mean that the mothers are sick. There are other reasons why mothers go to hospitals to have their babies.

For one thing, a mother needs a doctor and nurse to help her while her baby is being born. For another, it sometimes hurts a mother to give birth to a baby. And doctors and nurses can help to make things easier.

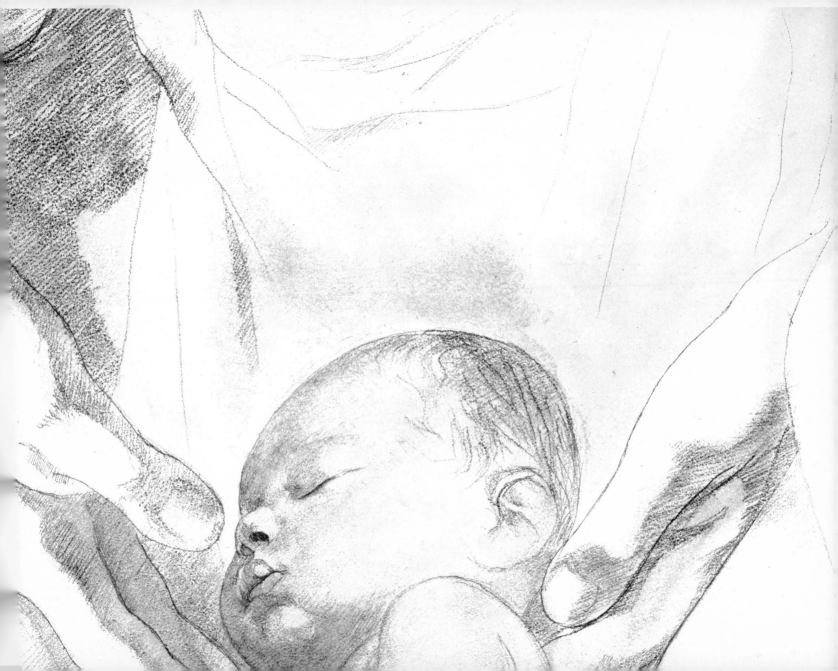

Most mothers don't mind the pain at all. This may sound strange to you. But giving birth to a baby is such a wonderful thing for a mother that the joy she feels is often much stronger than the pain. She is so excited because she is about to see her baby for the first time—the baby who was you and who had been alive but unseen inside her for so many months—that the pain is not so important.

Another reason for the doctor to be there is to take care of the baby after he is born and to listen for his first cry. Your first cry told the doctor that you were ready and able to breathe all by yourself.

The doctor also cuts the cord through which you got your food and air while you were in the womb. For a newborn baby is ready to take food through his mouth and to breathe through his nose and lungs all by himself. It doesn't hurt the mother when the cord is cut, or the baby either. All that is left to mark the place where the cord had been attached to the middle of your belly is your *belly button,* which is also called the *navel.*

You were a real baby then. And everybody wanted to see you. They asked all about you—how much you weighed, what your name was—and said how glad they were that you had come.

So—now you know how you lived in your mother's body before you were born and how you grew from a tiny fertilized ovum to be a baby.

And you know . . .

it takes a father as well as a mother to make a baby.

You know that every baby is born either a boy or a girl—that is, either male or female. You know that boys grow up to be men and girls grow up to be women. You also know that the bodies of boys and the bodies of girls are different from each other. A boy or a man has a *penis,* and a girl or a woman has a *vagina,* which is a passageway from a special opening between her legs that leads only to her womb. Both men and women have other parts *inside* their bodies that have to do with making babies. All these parts we call the sex or reproductive organs.

The sex organs inside a girl or woman are the womb and two special glands that store the tiny egg cells or ova. They are called *ovaries.* Each ovary is about as big as an olive. These two ovaries begin to release egg cells after a girl matures, when she reaches puberty—usually when she is between eleven and thirteen years old.

Every month an ovum leaves one of the two ovaries and travels through a tube leading to the womb, which is close by. On the way to the womb the ovum is ready to begin to grow into a baby. *But only if it is joined by something else.*

This very important something else is the *sperm* that comes from the father's body.

A man's body is different from a woman's. A man has two special sex organs that make sperm. They are inside a bag of skin hanging just behind his penis, and are called *testicles.* A man's testicles make many millions of sperm, but even though thousands are released at the same time, only one single sperm can enter the ovum and combine with it to begin a living, growing being.

You may find this hard to imagine, but the sperm that makes it possible for the ovum to grow into a baby is even smaller than the ovum—very much smaller! And of course nobody has ever seen sperm cells except through a microscope.

Through a microscope, a sperm looks something like the tadpoles you may have seen in brooks or ponds in the country. It has a long, thin, wiggling tail and a roundish little head. It swims about like a tadpole, too, with quick wrigglings of its tail.

As soon as a sperm enters an ovum, something amazing happens. The tiny little egg cell in the mother's body and the tiny little sperm cell from the father's body *join together.* They are no longer two separate things. They have become *one new* thing.

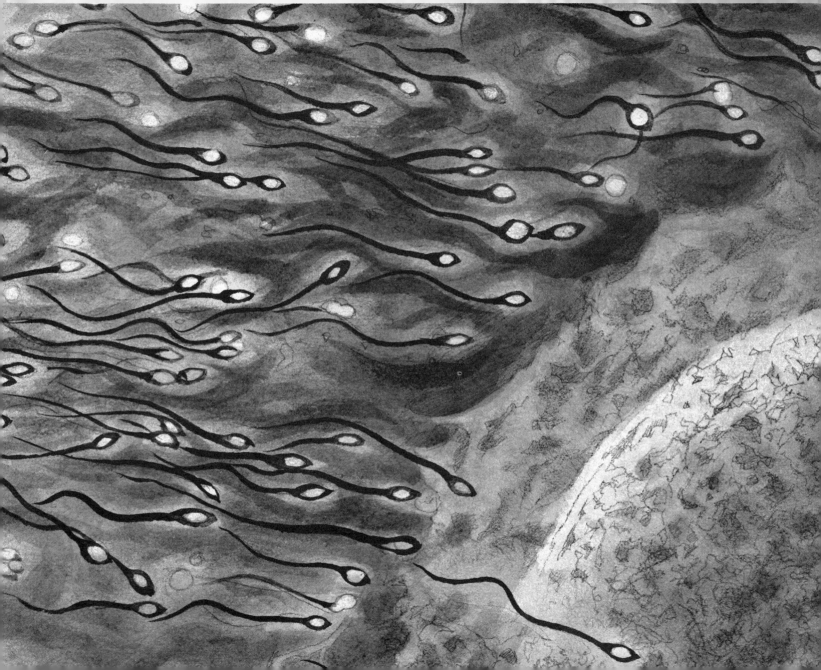

That one new thing is the ovum combined with the sperm, and it is really very different from the ovum by itself. It is a *fertilized* ovum. It is this fertilized ovum that develops into a baby.

The little ovum in your mother's body, by itself, was not you. And the little sperm in your father's body, by itself, wasn't you. *You* began to be only when the two joined together. That was the moment when you began to grow into a baby, and after that into a boy or girl, and later into the man or woman you will be someday.

In that first moment when the sperm and the ovum joined to make you, the question of whether you were going to be a girl or a boy was settled. That, and many, many other things—even the color of your hair and the color of your eyes.

Yes, all of these things were settled right there in the tiny fertilized ovum at the moment when the sperm and ovum united! That's another reason why everyone is full of wonder at the marvelous story of birth.

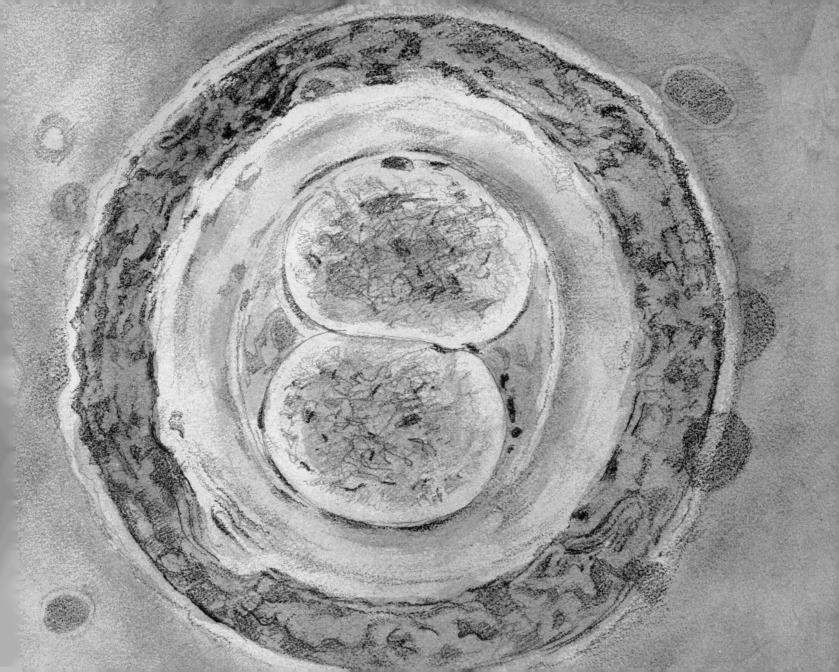

You began, then, only when something from your father's body joined something from your mother's body.

The sperm comes from the father's body through his penis. Waste water, or *urine,* passes through the penis too; but urine and sperm never pass through at the same time. A man's penis can fit into a woman's vagina, that passageway from an opening between her legs to her womb. In this way the sperm enter the body of the mother. They swim up the vagina through the womb and into the tubes. In one of the tubes an ovum might be moving toward the womb and might join with one of the millions of sperm deposited by the father.

You have a mother and a father. And everybody you know has a mother and a father. That's because they all began when a sperm and an ovum joined. The sperm came from the father, the ovum from the mother. That's why you may have eyes like your father's, but ears shaped like your mother's. That's why we may say you "take after" your father in some ways, even though you have grown inside your mother's body. That's why you may have a dimpled chin like your mother and a good singing voice like your father.

Sometimes people may even say you are "the image of" your grandfather. Or your grandmother. Or your mother's great-uncle Henry. Of course, this isn't *exactly* true. Because *you* only look like yourself, don't you? But it *is* true that you

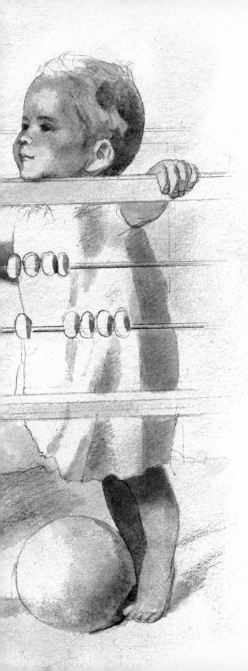

are more like other members of your family than you are like other people. This is because of the *particular* kind of sperm and egg that joined to make you. They not only made you resemble your mother and father in many ways, but your grandparents and other relatives as well. And, as a matter of fact, people you've never seen or heard of—your grandparents' parents and their grandparents. And so, far, far back to the time when people began.

Usually, only one human baby is born at a time, because one single egg cell leaves an ovary each month. But sometimes, two eggs leave at about the same time. Then it may happen that each one unites with a different sperm. If both fertilized egg cells grow into babies, they are called fraternal twins. One may be a boy and one a girl. They are like any other brother and sister. Or they may both be boys or both girls. Much more rarely, after a fertilized ovum starts to grow, it divides into two parts that are exactly the same; then each part can separately grow into a complete baby. These are called identical twins. Then the two babies are always either both girls or both boys. They are so much alike that usually even the mother and father cannot easily tell them apart. Do you know any twins?

Even more rarely, three or more eggs are fertilized. And then the mother may have triplets. Or, much more rarely quadruplets or quintuplets.

When you were an infant, you spent practically all of your time sleeping. You stayed awake just long enough to eat—and you woke up to do this every few hours. And every time you wanted to eat, somebody had to feed you. You couldn't do anything at all about it yourself. For you, like all human babies, were about the most helpless of all living things.

Human babies take a much longer time to grow up than babies of other kinds. Most of the animals you know best, like horses and dogs and cats and cows, are as big as their parents by the time they are two years old. A two-year-old dog can roam over the neighborhood all day long and take good care of himself. But a two-year-old baby cannot. As soon as it is born, a kitten can climb around its mother looking for the places to suck her milk. A human baby has to be held up to its mother's breast to nurse. Or if it nurses from a bottle, someone has to hold the bottle and put the nipple in the baby's mouth. A baby calf can stand on its own legs—even if they are pretty wobbly—the first day it is born. But you know it is a long time, often a whole year, before a human baby can stand up.

That's how it was for a long time after that great day when you were born; you couldn't do much more for your-self than breathe and eat—and grow. But every day you got bigger and stronger. And every day you became a little more able to make your muscles move the way you wanted them to. After a while you could turn your head to look at someone you heard coming into the room. Pretty soon you could smile at your mother and father, or anyone who looked at you. But it took a while before you could reach for a toy or hold your own bottle so that you could drink from it. Or laugh out loud when other children played with you.

But before your first birthday came around, you could pull yourself up to stand in your crib or your playpen. You could creep around on the floor and you could grab at everything you saw and get into everything you could reach. But you were still a baby.

Do you remember when you said Da-da instead of Daddy? Choo-choo instead of train? When you could ride a tricycle but not a bike? When you had to cry for something you wanted because you couldn't say the words to ask for it?

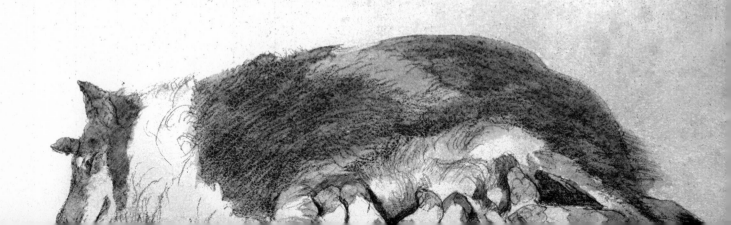

Now you are big and can do a great many things for yourself. You have grown and changed in very many ways. Because it is not only our bodies that grow and change. Our feelings grow and change, too, and we learn to understand more and more.

When you were a baby, you wanted to be near your mother all the time. Maybe you cried when she left you with someone else. Now you're just as happy playing away from home at a friend's house, aren't you?

First you needed to feel close mostly to your mother and father. Now you also enjoy feeling close to your friends. That's what is meant by saying that your feelings change as you grow older.

As you grow your body gets larger and stronger. It also changes in shape. You are able to do many more things with your body than you could do when you were a baby. Your feelings grow and change too. When you were still very young, you began to notice, and to wonder about your body, and about other people's bodies.

Sometimes a little girl feels terribly cheated because her brother has a penis. And so far as she can see, she has nothing at all. However, her brother may feel cheated too, even though he has a penis. He may feel that girls have all the luck; when they grow up, they can have babies but boys can't. Of course you know now how very important each is in his or her own way.

Human beings keep on learning and growing for a much longer time than animals do. As they grow up, boys and girls understand more with their minds and their feelings than any other animals. Men and women can read and write and think well enough to make up stories and songs and to invent airplanes. They can also feel a love for their children and for their husbands and wives that no other animals can. So, human beings live in families of fathers and mothers and children together.

You are growing and changing in your body and in your feelings all the time. In a few years, when you are twelve, thirteen, or fourteen, you will begin to grow even more quickly than you do now. That is the time when boys' bodies begin to change their shape and grow more like men's bodies, and their testicles begin to make sperm. Girls' bodies come to be more like women's bodies, and their ovaries begin to release ova.

As boys and girls become more grown-up, their feelings become more grown-up too. They begin to think about the changes in their bodies and about each other. They like to be with each other and go to dances and parties together. They are growing out of younger ways of loving, just as you grew out of needing your mother near you all the time. And they begin to wonder about grown-up ways of loving. They wonder about the future and think of the time when they will have children of their own and will give them all the kinds of love and care that children need.

Have you ever felt that good warm feeling of being close and together with other people? Of course you have. You have thrown your arms around your mother and hugged her tight, feeling very close to her.

When people are married, they feel very close to each other. A married man and woman feel this closeness with their hearts, and they also feel a special closeness with their bodies. They join their bodies together because they love each other. When they join their bodies, the man's penis enters the woman's vagina. That is how the sperm can fertilize the egg. Then the sperm and egg stop being two separate things and become one new thing—which is the beginning of a baby.

When a man and woman have children together, parents and children together become another kind of new thing. *This* new thing is a family.

Now you know how the story goes. You know how the ovum and the sperm join together. You know how the tiny fertilized ovum begins to grow. You know how it changes from a little egg cell that could hardly be seen, and grows bigger, and changes into a baby inside the mother. And you know how the baby is born, and how it grows from a little thing in its crib to be a boy or girl as big as you are.

And you are still growing. Little boys and girls become big boys and girls. Then they become men and women, and get married and have children of their own. Their children grow up and have more children, and *they* have children—and so on and on like a story that never comes to an end.

It's such an interesting story that we always want to know more about it. As you grow older, you'll have many other

questions. You'll want to understand more about yourself, your body, and your feelings.

And all this is part of the same wonderful story—the most wonderful story in the world—the *true* story of how you were born.